Naming The Days

Sakthi

First Published in 2021

Becomeshakespeare.com

One Point Six Technologies Pvt Ltd

119-123, 1st Floor, Building J2, B-Wing,
Wadala Truck Terminal, Wadala (East),
Mumbai 400022, Maharashtra, India

T: +91 8080226699

ISBN - 978-93-5458-096-3

To my aunt

Rukmani

Table of Contents

Parenting — 55

Naming — 67

Nature — 79

I

Digital Love

Facebook

Facebook is a book of our memories
You can also say face book is a
Face and
Book for our memories
The extension of our mind
The extension of human mind

As we post a post in the Facebook
We like to receive likes and comments from our friends
We have so many friends
Our so many friends have so so many many friends

Our post is one among the many many post on their walls
On their Facebook page
On their memories
On their mind

We expect importance for our post
Likewise

Our friends expect importance for their post

Some times we scroll every post
We run through all comments
We run behind to get likes and comments for our post

Friendships are reduced to following the friend's post
Feelings are reduced to Emojis
Human beings are reduced to comments

As we equate words and comments with human beings
Whether known one or unknown one
We ready for the fight
To protect our image
Our ideologies
Our identities

Are our identities are just a Facebook page
Are our identity is just our face and book of our memories

Can you sense a human being beyond their face and book
of the memories?

Romantic movies

Romantic movies
Most admired genre among
Other genre movies

Most admired because
It gives a sense of dream come true
The sense of fulfilment
The sense of aliveness
In a boring routine life

What a liberation to fall in love
To feel complete
And to forget ourselves with
All the cute scenes of
Romance in love
Like
The love scenes of romantic movies
Romances are the movies

Epic love stories of all time

Life seems wasted if we have not fallen in love

Fallen in love with ourselves

Fallen in love with our dream lover

Fallen in love with our dream

We always romanticise the time

Seek fulfilment in time

Fall in love with time

Though

We already know romantic movies are illusion

We still allow ourselves to fall in love

Fall in love with romantic movies of our time and

All time

The same way we know seeking fulfilment in time

Is illusion

We always allow ourselves to fall in love with our time and
all time

With our time in all the time

With time

We fall from love all the time

We fall from love all the time

Role playing

We all are hero in our own life
We own the life like a movie hero.

Mass movie hero
Either play
Lover or
Victim or
Villain

Sometimes with possibility and probability of those three roles
In all the possible permutations and combinations

Victim of life situations is the most favourite of all three
Victim of love
Victim of villains actions
Victim of our own victim identity

Victim of victim

Is the most seductive of all

We can give all the reasons for any question
That questions our victim identity

We like to be a hero
Who has relationships with the above roles

We can't be a real hero
who creates the real change
Within himself and others
If we play the roles

Our mass movie hero
Always plays the roles
That we easily lose ourselves
So that
We can forget ourself
Our true self
And become one with the movie

Digital life

We all live in a digital age

Most advanced and miraculous technologies are at our fingertips

We can connect to it any moment

Mostly we connect to it all the time

Knowingly or unknowingly

As you connect with the gadgets

You connect with the world

You connect your mind with

The collective mind

Like the world

Technology is neither good or bad

As we walk around the world

We are careful

If we are not careful

We may expose ourselves to harm
So with technologies

With technologies
We are flooded with too much information all the time
More than what we need
More than what we want

Then we assume our lives is out there in gadgets
We lose ourselves in digital images
We miss what surrounds us

We experience our world through gadgets
Looking at a tree and
Looking at a digital image of a tree
Become same for us and it
Becomes norm for us

For us and
For our children
There is a difference in age
Actually and digitally

Digital addiction is progressively progressing

Without a balance of real and digital
Our life becomes outdated and problematic

With
Continuous noises
Continues voices
In our head
In our gadgets
Our life becomes hyperactive

The voice in the head keeps on activating
Noise in the world
In turn
Noise in the world amplifies
Voice in the head

Till we find the balance
Within ourself
Till we find our true self within ourself
Our life remains problematic

Turnoff the noises of gadgets
Turn away from the voice in the head

Tune into silence every now and then both
Within and without

To remain sane
Within and without
Tune into silent space in and around you

Silence is sane
Noise is insane

To remain sane
Within and without
Tune into silent space in and around you

Selfie

If
You
Take
Photo of
Yourself
By yourself
For yourself
It is a
Selfie

Look
Pose
Feel
The
Same way

Same way
You
Take

Selfie

Different
Faces
Different
Poses
For
Different
Selfie
To show
Your
Uniqueness

Uniqueness
Falls into
Unique
Pattern

Pattern
Is same
Selfies are
Different

Pattern

Is same

Selfies are

Different

Becoming popular

Becoming popular is so easy and

So fast in the new age

In the new age

Becoming unpopular is also so easy and so fast

With modern age technologies

Time and distance no longer exists

Virtually

As if

Time and distance never exists

Message spreads in an instant

Everyone gets to know everything about you

Before you know about you

Before you know about you

Everyone gets to know about

You status

Your value

Your personal life
So easily

As you become popular
Managing and maintaining
Your personal life
Your image value and
Your status
Are not easy

As you gain something you lose something

A single tweet
A single post
A single word
A single moment
Can bring you down
So easily
A single moment
Can bring down your image value
Instantly
So connected we are

We are not living in the time of letters

You need not wait for a long time

To put your message across

To put your image across

Everything was slow and followed its own rhythm

Now rhythm is there

Unnaturally super fast

You can go up and

Down

In an instant

As you gain something you lose something

As you lose something you gain nothing

As you lose something

You gain no thing

In the end you gain

No

Thing

Watching the movies

Watching the movies
Watching the making of movies
Watching the making of making
We all addicted to movie watching

We all like
To trace and track the process of making
It's story writing
It's screen play
It's direction
It's audition and edition

Watching the movies
Watching the news
Keep us informed
Keep us entertained
So that we are not uneasy with ourselves
So that we are not easy with ourselves

So we invent lot of

Gadgets to keep us occupied

Smart phone is our small television

Now

We can occupy ourselves in any where in any time

In any given time we are occupied

In any given time we occupy our time

In any given time we are pre occupied with time

In any given time we are pre occupied with time

In now

We can occupy ourselves from any where from any time

Without time

We occupy the time

Falling in love

Looking
For
A
Life
Partner

Falling
In
Love

Romantic
Love
Puppy
Love

Falling
In
Love

Fall
From
Love

Why
This
Fall

We like
So much
The
Dream
Of
Falling
In
Love

So
We keep
Falling
Again
And
Again

Dream

Love

Dream

Life

Continue

To

Run

Our

Life

Till

We

Are

In a

Dream

Dream

Continues

As

Long

As

We

Sleep

When
We
Wake up
No
Dream
Love
No
Dream
Life

Only
Life

Dance of stars

Dance of stars
Twitter wars
All the stars
Stars of politicians
Stars of sportsman
Stars of people
Stars of protagonist
Stars of antagonist
Participate in the
War of stars
It is Star Wars

Everyone one jumps in
To dance as soon as they get a chance to dance
As everyone jumps in
The pool of water
It becomes the muddy water

Nothing is clear

Who is right

Who is wrong

Who dances well

Who doesn't dance well

It is like a street dance

You can see and feel the

Rhythms and movements of

Beat

You also move to dance in this grand feast of

Star Wars

War of stars

In Twitter

In face book

In all the social media

All records this street dance of stars

Star Wars is a street dance of stars

To dance like a real star

To shine like a real star

Be the observer of all the drama

Of human emotions

Of human lives
As you be the observer
You become a real star

As you be the observer
You become the real star

Error of terror

Terror hero
Heroine is in terror

Men or women we all like the
Terror hero who is teasing a
Terrified heroine

There is an error
The way we all like this
Terror

Following
Attracting
Attacking
Defending and
Abusing
Nature of masculine
Running
Escaping

Nature of feminine
Like a war hunt in an enemy territory

Men or women
All prefer
Masculine nature over the
Feminine nature

We prefer the error of terror
Till we prefer the terror
We never solve the error

To resolve the error
See the error of terror
See the error as error

To resolve the error
See the error of terror
See the error as error

Virtual living

Loving and living directly
Loving and living indirectly

Directly
You meet in person
You meet the person
To have a real connection

Indirectly
You meet them online
You meet their image
On virtual screen
You form a connection with virtual image

Watching the tree directly
Watching the tree on a screen
On screen
You can see only the image

Online classes are interactions of images
Interactions are
Like a river that left dry on a hot summer

What you see on the screen is not a reality
What you see is not the reality

You left with
Glaring screen
Soaring eyes
Drying throat
You suffocate
Like a travel in a heavily loaded
Heavily crowded bus

You long for a fresh air
Deeply
Internally
But all the glamorous attractions of
Screen personalities
External sensory pleasures
Still pulls you to go for more rides
On the heavily loaded bus

How long

How many more rides

We like to do the same trip

With heavy loads of stuff on our heads

In the crowded bus

Stop interacting only virtually

Give full stop to non stop online classes

Take a break

Walk to a park

Hug a tree

Watch the sky

Feel the breeze

Smell the flowers

Listen to the silence

All you ever need

Ever need to know

Ever need to learn are already there

Around you and

Within you

Be there as a witnessing presence
Witnessing presence of
All around you
All of you

You learn
You know
You live
Much more fully
Than endless staring of screen with your
Soaring red eyes

Give a break
Take a walk

All you ever need
Ever need to know
Ever need to learn are already there
Around you and
Within you

Be there as a witnessing presence
Witnessing presence of

All around you

All of you

Dove in love

Why dove is a symbol of love?

To represent the
Freedom in love?

Are we free in our love?
Or
Are we clinging to each other for the love?

If we cling
Does that real love?

Our culture is full of love songs
Love movies
Whatever is forbidden in the society
We seek them through the movies

Virtual movies

Mental movies

In love

Each one is dove

Both can fly freely in the sky

One can return to their nest when it wants to

They can fly anytime if they want to

Doves are in understanding

Not of compulsion

Living in the relationships

Living the relationships

Living relationships

We know dove is a symbol of love

We love only symbolically

We never love

We never live

Like a symbol of love

To be like a symbol of love

To be a symbol for the love

Follow the simple love of the dove

To be a symbol for the love

Follow the simple love of the dove

Drama of love

The template of love in movies
The template of love songs
The template of love
Same across all movies

We relish and cherish the same repetition of
Falling in love
Being in love
In our movies
In our minds

Lovely bubbly innocent girl
Manly boldly killer boy
Either boy chase the girl or girl chase the boy
Then love hate relationship begins
The drama begins
Never ending ego clashes begins

We love to watch their play on screen

We love to play roles like the hero and heroines of love movies

As if we are the hero and heroine of the movies

Romance moments are

Romantic movements are

Flying in the air

Deep longing deep wanting looks

Can't miss the partner even for a moment

Lovely love game

Between the two

In each one of the two

There is a two

One is lover

Other is hater

Lover in oneself loves the lover in other
Hater in oneself hates the hater in other
Sometimes
Lover in oneself loves the hater in other
Hater in oneself loves the hater in other

Sometimes
Above four options are in oneself
Likewise
In the other

The drama of love hate relationships
Complex drama of human relationships

When all the drama ends
Love begins

When all the drama of the mind ends
Love begins

Online

Online
Classes
Goes
On
Line

Goes
On
Line

Line
Connects
One
To
Many

Does
Many
Connect

To

One

If

Many don't

Connect

To

One

One

Can't

Connect

To

Many

Distance

Furthers

By

Distance

Though

Connection

Is

There

There

Is

No

Connection

No

Connection

To

Presence

To

Sense

Their

Full

Presence

Online

Goes

Like

Hole

Within

A

Hole

Hole

Can't

Connect

To

Whole

Only

Presence

Can

Connect

To the

Whole

Fully

Hole

Can't

Connect

To the

Whole

Fully

Soulfully

II

Parenting

Parenting is a

Parenting is a spiritual practice
Retreat centre is your home
Spiritual teachers are your children
You are the seeker

Don't waste time in following any path
Don't run behind any guru
Don't sit in cushion for the countless hours
Don't wish for any spiritual experience
Don't worry about the enlightenment

All is at home
At free of cost

Practice is the day to day tasks in daily life
Children are the mirror for your progress
As you progress
In the path
Your mirror your children

You see the error of your mirror

As you progress
In the path
Your mirror your children
You see the error of your mirror

ABCD

Say
'Hi'
To
Uncle

Say
'ABCD'
Say
'123'
Say
This
Do
That

We
Say
To
Little
Ones

Little

One

Say

One

Two

Three

ABCD

To

Older

Ones

Till

They

Grow up

To

Say

Say

123

ABCD

To

Their

Little

Ones

Your child is you

We get angry on our children
For their small small mischiefs

One spiritual teacher said
Children are our spiritual teachers
Parenting is a spiritual practice

They teach patience
As if they won't leave us
Until we become patient

They actually show our impatience
They test our limits
They are the
Masters of adult students

They sometimes pull our legs knowingly
Many times unknowingly
To show our inherent limitations

To point to our limitless potentials

They are our unmet businesses
They won't leave us
Until we meet our unmet businesses

Our
Unmet need for the kindness
Unmet need for unconditional love
Unmet need for acceptance of who we are as we are

They are the pointers for the direction for our self discovery
There may be a time you hate your masters
There may be a time you love your masters

In your self discovery
You discover they are yourself
You are meeting your self
As if time fades from memory

You are your child
Your child is you

When time fades from memory

You are your child

Your child is you

Children

Being a parent is like being a
Captain of the ship

Being a captain of the ship
You need to have the skills and confidence in your own
abilities to navigate through an
Uncharted sea

To navigate through an uncharted sea
You need to anchor within yourself
Your deeper self

As you go deeper within yourself
You know more about you

As you know more about you
You know more about your child
The reason for your child's behaviour in any given moment

In any giving moment by being aware of your self

Aware of your actions and reactions

You sense the root cause

The source of your child's behaviour

Your child is here to point out all your unmet needs and emotions within yourself

Which you push down

Within yourself for so long

You don't know how long

But

Your child is here to push the button to bring up all that you hold deep down

All that you pressed down

Within your self

Parenting is a spiritual practice

Children are the spiritual teachers

They are here to awaken you

As you awaken

You see them as yourself

As you awaken

You see them as yourself

III

Naming

Sense the life

Posters in a garden
Names of the plants
Names of the trees
Names of the flowers
With the full knowledge of botany

The not so easy botanical names
Why do we need to know all those
To sense the life in the garden
To sense the life of the garden

We are stuck with names and forms
That dulls the freshness of flowers
Dew drops on the leaves
Swaying trees
Cool breeze
Smell of the soil

To sense the life of the garden

We don't need to know the names and forms

To sense the life in all life

We don't need to know the names and forms

Never ending

Full

Health

Check

Up

Check

Your

Blood pressure

Sugar level

Pulse

Rate

Everything

Is

Rate

Each

Organ

Has

It's

Own

Rate

Countless

Names

Countless

Diseases

Countless

Patients

Countless

Treatments

For the

Human

Body

Body's

Structure

Is

Same

Names

Are

Countless

So

Choices

For

Business

Are

Countless

Our

Busy ness

Our

Dis easy ness

Creates

Lot of

Business

Busy ness

Business

Diseases

Dis easy ness

Never ending

Cycle of

Side effects

Side effects

Never

Ends

Circle

Never

Ends

End

The

Circle

Now

Otherwise

You

End

In

Never ending

Cycle

Never ending

Circle

Naming the days

Endless thirst to name every day
To give special to day to day
To give special effects to day to day life

Mother's day
Father's day
Lover's day
Birthday
Freedom day
Are we really free
From the oppressions and depressions
From the endless hunger for this and that
Endless hunger to fill our days with names

Why this endless hunger and thirst to fill our days?

The only name to name a day we left is death day
We are yet to find a way to celebrate our own death day
We are yet to discover our way for that

To discover a way even for that
When we discover a way for that
We can even go further
We only go further
Only when we stop naming
Stop shaming the inherent beauty of simple day to day

To decorate a simple day with artificial flowers
Artificial wishes and kisses
We dull our nature
We are immature as we fill and full our days with plastic
elastic names

As we fill and full the nature with everlasting plastic
So we fill our true nature with
Elastic and plastic

Within so without

Happiness is

The culture of happy weekends
Then what about the week days?

Weekdays are for the commitments
To live the live for others
Weekends are for ourselves

Weekdays are more than the weekends
In the number of days
In the number of days
We are unhappy in more days than the happy days

We always look for the happy days
Once the weekend ends
As weekend anyway ends in 'end'
We look for the next weekend
We earn and wait for the next happy day

If we are not happy today

We are not happy tomorrow

Because tomorrow also comes as today

Yesterday is the last day

Tomorrow is the next day

Yesterday is the last today

Tomorrow is the next today

Happiness is in the moment

Happiness is this moment

Only this moment

IV

Nature

If we left

Noon breeze

Dancing leaves

Chirping birds

Standing trees

Quietness of Afternoon

In cool shade

Sitting on park bench

Writing a poem

Life is blessing

If left alone

If we left

Life

Alone

Everywhere

Let the trees, flowers, birds, sky and stars speak to you

Connect with nature
In such a way you can listen to them

Listen to the mountain stream
Listen to the chirping birds
Listen to your breathing
Listen quietly the silence beneath all of them

Listen to the silence beneath the silence
Stillness that emanates from the silence

Having connection with nature
Connecting with your true nature are
One and the same

As you connect with nature

You connect with your true nature

Connect with nature till the connection with nature becomes

Your second nature

Then

Nature becomes your second nature

Nature is every where

So you are everywhere

Nature is every where

So you are everywhere

Flying

I'm forced and confined to a
Room
Longing for a
Fresh Air
Sunshine
Dew drops
Like a
Grass that
Dances with a
Breeze

Like to fly like a bird
If I have the wings
I want to
Break this cage
To fly
Freely

Cloud less sky

Waiting for me

Cloud less sky

Yearning for me

Cloud less sky

Calling for me

To

Fly

How did I get confined to

This

Room

Only

To this

Room

It is suffocating

Can I have a small hole

At least

To see

The

Cloud less sky

When I look for a hole

Surprisingly

I found a window

That

Opens to the

Vastness of sky

Calling

When I see the cloud less sky

I forget myself

And

This

Room

I

Become

A bird

That is

Flying

Just flying

Not having a

Sense of

It

Is

Flying

Just flying

Human beings are

Human beings are finished products or work in progress?

How come universe creates a specie that destroys itself?

Something wrong here?

To wonder the creations of the universe

Look at the night sky

To wonder the creativity of the universe

Look at the nature

To wonder

Look at the evening sky

Look at the morning flower

Look at the summer fruit

Look at the winter night

Look at puppy's face

Look at baby's smile

How come universe creates a specie that destroys itself?

Something wrong here?
Wrong here
If human beings are finished products

If human beings are finished products
Then
No hope
No escape

If human beings are finished products
Then
No hope
No escape

Without words

Can you talk without words?
Can you communicate in silence?
Can you communicate with silence?
Can you listen to the silent conversations?

Swaying sayings of the trees
Dancing flowers
Murmurings of a gentle breeze
The bird's call
The animal's sound
River's music
Earth's silence
All is communicating
To all

To listen to all
Do you need words and
Languages?

To communicate to all

Do you need words and

Languages?